THE *Wisdom* OF
Yo Meow Ma

A SPIRITUAL GUIDE FOR LIVING A BETTER LIFE

JOANNA SANDSMARK

CARROLL & BROWN PUBLISHERS LIMITED

猫
哲
学

For Art, Emalou, Bill, Tim, Madonna, Nancy & Mouse,
and for my own Yo Meow Ma, Trace.

First published in 2005 in the United Kingdom by

Carroll & Brown Publishers Limited
20 Lonsdale Road London NW6 6RD

Text © Joanna Sandsmark 2005
Illustrations Daniel Egneus/Thorogood Illustration
Compilation © Carroll & Brown Limited 2005

A CIP catalogue record for this book is available from the British Library.

ISBN 1-904760-03-1

10 9 8 7 6 5 4 3 2 1

Reproduced by RDC, Malaysia
Printed and bound by Artes Graficas Toledo, Spain

Contents

Introduction

How It All Began

In 1974, I was going through my morning routine with only a fraction of my mind engaged by the newscast blaring in the background when my attention was suddenly captured by the story of a stunning discovery – a mysterious find deep in the heart of China. A graphic showed a sandstone wall with what appeared to be meaningless scratches, lines of ochre, and the occasional paw print.

Archaeologists had uncovered a sandstone burial chamber deep in the heart of the Takla Maklan Desert in northwestern China. Once a part of the "Silk Road," the area has yielded several spectacular archaeological finds in recent history. When the team broke into the untouched tomb they found the remains of a naturally mummified cat (i.e. mummified through the arid forces of nature, not by any human process). Although mummified cats are common in Egypt, they are highly unusual in China.

And there were more surprises. Within the tomb were several bundles of scrolls. When one was carefully unrolled, the scientists were fascinated to discover it was covered with scratches, bites, ochre lines, and paw prints. They appeared to have been "written" by a cat! Further exploration of the tomb yielded more scratches, bites, lines, and prints etched and painted onto the walls. The archaeologists were unsure what to make of them, but vowed to explore their mysteries.

My mind vibrated with the implications of the story I had just seen. I was young – barely out of college – and had been toying with the idea of taking a year off to travel instead of going straight to grad school. The discovery of the cat tomb decided my destiny. I needed to go to China.

I sold my car and most of my possessions, and cashed in my savings to finance the trip. My youth and lack of graduate degrees would afford me little respect in scientific circles, but I was determined to see the tomb for myself. I couldn't put my finger on exactly what it was, but I knew that somehow, the random-looking scratches, bites, lines, and paw-prints felt like they held a deeper meaning.

That was the beginning of my life's obsession. After visiting China, and taking a prodigious amount of photographs of the tomb walls, the sarcophagus, the mummy, and the scrolls, I returned to the University to get my Master's degree in linguistics, and a Ph.D. in the field I helped create: Catosophy – the study of cat philosophy. For when I had finally looked upon those sandstone scratchings with my own eyes, I knew instantly that there was nothing random or meaningless about them. These were messages, sent to us by a feline intellect thousands of years in the past.

The Writings

By now, you probably realize that the tomb was that of Yo Meow Ma, the most famous feline philosopher in history. All of the subsequent finds – the Kyoto Cat, the Ganges Cat, Great Britain's "Shakespeare's Shadow", the United States' Lesser Mouser, Thor's Cat, the Aztec Cat, and even the Pharaoh's Cat – pale in comparison to the wealth that was buried in the sands of the Takla Maklan Desert. Whereas the most prodigious of her rivals, Mexico's Aztec Cat, wrote 14 rules for living, Yo Meow Ma wrote enough to fill several books.

One of the most valuable gifts that the Yo Meow Ma Collection brought to us was the legacy of learning she passed onto her students. The translated passages taken from the walls of the tomb all begin with the phrase "The Mouser says," in reference to her status as the enlightened Master. This tells us that Yo Meow Ma did not write the text found on the sandstone walls. This was written by successive generations of students and was most likely part of a ritualistic tribute to the deceased master.

The scrolls, on the other hand, do not have a similar introduction and are believed, therefore, to have been written by the paws of Yo Meow Ma herself. The "flavor" of the scrolls is distinctly different from the lessons found on the walls. There is a boldness to the patterns, bites, and scratches that the student writings lack. Yo Meow Ma's strength of character and her confidence are illustrated with every stroke. Having spent the past 30 years of my life learning the intricacies of her language, the subtlety of her markings still has the power to astound me.

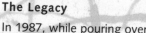

The Legacy

In 1987, while pouring over a scroll written by the Kyoto Cat, a somewhat startling theory popped into my mind. "What if Yo Meow Ma was the true originator?" Could it be that Yo Meow Ma was the first of the philosopher cats, and that all others learned from her? After putting together clues and evidence, everything fell into place. In retrospect, it all seemed so obvious that I wondered why it had taken so long to figure it out.

The accepted view today is that Yo Meow Ma was indeed the true originator. She created the language, wrote the initial allegories, lessons, and axioms, and all other cats learned from her.

Her students spread her word to other cats, who then told more, who told still more, and so on. This explains why we have found so many similar lessons and allegories despite enormous geographical barriers. How could the Aztec Cat, far off in the undiscovered New World, write 14 scrolls that were virtually identical to the Pharaoh's Cat in Egypt? And why were the Pharaoh's Cat's lessons the same as those written by Yo Meow Ma in her scrolls?

Obviously, cats were communicating on a grand scale. This was unthinkable before the discovery of Yo Meow Ma's tomb, but we now understand that felines across the planet speak a single, uniform language, and share a remarkable set of philosophies initiated by the one they uniformly call "The Mouser" – Yo Meow Ma.

Cats today continue to write and speak to each other in the same ways as their ancestors. Every time one scratches a piece of furniture, bites the edges of a piece of paper, or tracks muddy paw prints, he is, in fact, communicating universal messages to anyone able to understand.

The Interpreters

In your hands is the culmination of my love affair with the writings of Yo Meow Ma. Each passage has been painstakingly translated, and only those that have earned the consensus of my esteemed colleagues and other experts in the field are printed in this text. I have left those passages where debate still remains for another time. I want you to know that the lessons you are reading are, in fact, the words of the immortal Yo Meow Ma, and not just some catosopher's wishful thinking.

The Three Forms

Some of scrolls contained allegories. These are fascinating for their glimpses into the lives of the cats who inhabited The Mouser's world. Unlike her sayings and axioms, the allegories are told in story form, and teach very clear lessons based on the actions and life experiences of cats she either met or heard about. Other scrolls appeared to contain straight lessons. There also was a scroll titled "Axioms" that was a collection of pithy sayings. The combination of the allegories, lessons, and axioms gives a well-rounded roadmap toward living a better life, or, as The Mouser herself puts it, "...the search for felightenment." Yo Meow Ma covered a great range of subjects, only some of which are reprinted in this volume.

Although all of her messages are aimed at cats, and use the world of the cat to teach, I've yet to find even one that cannot be interpreted to fit the human world. I feel that this is, in fact, the true brilliance of Yo Meow Ma. Her words and teachings transcend her species, and speak of universal truths from which every animal on the planet could learn.

To aid you in your discovery of her teachings, I have included my own analysis, where appropriate, in an attempt to translate the teachings into human terms. It is my hope that, like the students who passed on the word of The Mouser to other students, I, too, can be a conduit between you and her Word.

It is astonishing to think that a cat could have tapped into so much of what the universe is about, but just as there are humans that transcend the ordinary – like Einstein, Newton, Mozart, Confucius, and Plato – so will there occasionally be cats who reach far beyond their species' limitations. Yo Meow Ma managed to cross the barriers of time and communication, and has done just that.

I hope that you enjoy the teachings of Yo Meow Ma. Or, to use the words of The Mouser herself,

"Be a cat who is never satisfied with smallness. Be instead one who learns in each of your nine lives."

The Bird-bound Cat

❝The cat with a taste for birds will jump higher than those who hunger only for mice. For the mouse-bound cat, the world is only the ground. For the bird-bound cat, the ground marries the sky and they are one. Cats were born to leap taller than the largest dog, so why does the mouse-bound cat enforce false limitations?

I answer you with this thought: be true to your nature, yet not content with it. You have four paws and no wings. Let that not deter you from using those paws to leap from mother earth to father sky, for then you are the wing-ed, and the bird is your lunch. ❞

As is typical with some of Yo Meow Ma's later work, this lesson begins with an introduction that could stand alone. "The cat with a taste for birds" represents all that you can achieve in your life. If you already aspire to things that can seem impossible or at the very least, difficult to capture, then you are a cat with a taste for birds. However, most people resemble the mouse-bound cat – you are content only to chase those dreams that are easily attainable and safe, and do not aspire to be more than your own self-imposed construct.

Yo Meow Ma is careful not to denigrate the mouse-bound cat; she acknowledges that you have no wings, and are therefore not meant to fly. But you do have the ability to leap at opportunity, and it is this aspect of your nature that she is illuminating in this lesson. For example, you may have a job that allows you to make ends meet. It may not be exciting or what you dreamed you'd do as a child, but it is safe and familiar. Yet when you are alone, you may think about those things that you did dream about in your youth. Perhaps you had a talent that you allowed to lie fallow, or maybe you aspired to a career that circumstances didn't allow you to pursue.

Yo Meow Ma is not suggesting you quit your job and immerse yourself in financial distress. Her use of the phrase "the ground marries the sky and they are one," clearly shows that the bird-bound cat doesn't only look skyward for sustenance. She eats mice, too. The point is that she does not limit herself only to food that is easily captured. In this way, you can become a bird-bound cat by opening your eyes to the opportunities around you. You can "marry" your current circumstances to future dreams and strive to have both security and the adventure of chasing what your heart desires.

Another interpretation, first put forward by Dr. Richard Bast (well-known author and professor of catosophy at the University of Wisconsin) suggests that Yo Meow Ma is telling her students to pursue every goal, regardless of its grandeur, as if it is a bird. "... be true to your nature, yet not content with it" does lend itself to Dr. Bast's theory. Being true to yourself, regardless of circumstances, is an incredibly important part of a well-balanced mind. Living only in fantasy can destroy whatever promise you might have, as it tends to infuse fear and avoidance into anything that is too "real."

The brilliance of Yo Meow Ma comes through with the addendum "yet not content with it," as here she shows that you can be true to yourself, your circumstances, and the practicalities of your life, without sentencing yourself to a life of non-aspiration. In short, it is okay to be who you are, yet continue to dream of being more. In fact, it's not just okay; it is desired. For then, and only then, will you be a bird-bound cat.

When you run from what
frightens you, remember that the
higher you climb, the thinner
the branch.

The Story of Yao Lee

Yao Lee was a lazy cat, who aspired to nothing more than long naps and food left to him by humans. Yet he did not pay these humans with purrs and cuddles. When they brought him food, he hissed, then ate his fill. Yao Lee turned his back on hunting. He claimed that some day he would learn, but now he needed rest.

One day, the humans did not come, and Lee's belly remained empty. He wailed and screamed but no food appeared. Perilously hungry, he invaded the territory of other cats, begging their scraps. Scratches and bites were his reward. Despondent, he stretched out on sandy ground, preparing to die.

A wandering old tom, Long Fang, came upon him, and asked him why he did not hunt to fill his belly. Yao Lee admitted he had put off learning for so long that he no longer knew where to begin.

Fang glanced at a nearby bush and told him that mice lived within the roots. "Pounce, and you will feed."

Yao Lee responded, "Today I am too weary. Tomorrow I will pounce."

Fang said, "For a lifetime you have been saying these words. Is tomorrow not arrived?"

Yao Lee's empty belly agreed with the tom, so he rose shakily to his feet. But too many tomorrows had passed, and he died before he reached the bush. Long Fang kept Yao Lee's lesson forever in his mind. The saying, "Do not delay, what can be done today" are the words of Long Fang. This story he told to me, and I tell it now to you.

To me, one of the more fascinating aspects of this story is Yo Meow Ma's acknowledgment of the obligations between pets and humans. The humans obviously did their part, by feeding the lazy cat. But Yao Lee did not keep his end of the bargain. "Yet he did not pay these humans with purrs and cuddles. When they brought him food, he hissed, and then ate his fill," shows us that The Mouser is aware that one of the primary reasons humans keep cats as pets is for their companionship, i.e. their "purrs and cuddles." By not keeping his part of this unspoken bargain, it is Yao who is painted in the negative, and not the humans (who did, after all, stop feeding him). There is no mention of why the humans disappeared, nor is there any condemnation of them for their abandonment.

Our own lives show us that if we do not contribute equally in a relationship, then that relationship can be built on a shaky foundation. Whether you give too much or too little, the inequities can strain the fabric enough that both parties feel it. If it eventually breaks, it is usually the taker, rather than the giver, who appears in a more negative light.

The truth, however, is that both parties must share responsibility for the breakdown of a relationship. Inequity on either end is still inequity. If you are playing the role of "taker" in a relationship, it is clear that you must work harder and be more generous with your time and attention, if you want it to work. But if you are filling the role of "giver" then you also have work to do. It might be time to question why you are in such a lopsided relationship, and what benefits you are getting from your unanswered generosity. Are you trying to buy love? Are you clinging to this other person because he or she fulfills some need, and therefore it's worth the "price" you are paying?

If you are uncomfortable with a one-sided relationship, it's up to you to find the balance you desire. Whether you do this through discussion with the other party, or you become more aware of your needs in the relationship, or even if you decide to sever your ties – you must take the first step. Don't leave your happiness in the hands of others.

Yao Lee allowed others to determine whether he would live or die. He put off taking his own destiny in his hands by refusing to learn to hunt. And he took without giving when he accepted the human's care while reacting to it with animosity. His mistakes ended in his death, obviously the most serious of all consequences. But your similar mistakes could end in the death of a relationship that you cherish and wish to retain.

Take Yao Lee's example to heart and examine your own interpersonal relationships to see if they are balanced.

The Invading Cat

"The invading cat thinks only his ways are the right ways, and those who do not follow his actions have no rights. If he sees a cat doing things differently, or believing what he does not believe, he invades his territory, feeling it his duty to set the other straight. As all cats know, your territory is your most important possession. A cat without territory uses his nine lives in the space of one. Without territory, he cannot hunt, and without hunting he starves. The invading cat often thinks he knows best. He thinks that his way of hunting, grooming, mating, or patrolling is the only way. He considers himself better than other cats and that is why he crosses into land that is not his, to take from another what he could not achieve. The invading cat is never satisfied, for there will always be cats who think differently than him, or do things in a different manner. Guard yourself from the invading cat. You are the master of your territory, not another. You determine how to hunt, groom, mate, or patrol. If you allow the invading cat to steal your territory, you will be the wanderer. And then where will you hunt? In your heart you know that there is room for many kinds of hunting, grooming, mating, and patrolling. In your heart you know that the invading cat is not helping you. He is trying to take what is not his: your thoughts and your territory. **"**

The lesson entitled "The Invading Cat" sounds like it might apply only to cats. With its emphasis on territory and hunting rights, many humans of today's world might think there is nothing to be learned from the passage.

Instead of seeing territory in the literal sense, as a cat might, expand it to mean anything that is yours that you are unwilling to share. Note that in all of The Mouser's examples, none of the things taken are given willingly. She isn't talking about the things in your life that you would willingly share or give to another. She is talking about the things that make you you: your thoughts, beliefs, relationships, and family.

Yet she is also speaking in a literal sense. You wouldn't welcome a thief into your home, or smile happily if someone stole your car, or kidnapped your children. One must be careful to protect those things that are important.

What of generosity, you may ask? This passage doesn't deal with what you would willingly give. It speaks only to those things that might be taken forcibly.

The passage made me think of an ex-colleague of mine when I was a guest professor at Arthur Ray University. He resented me joining the department, yet he gave the appearance of being welcoming. To my face, he was always polite, and appeared to care about my opinions. Yet no matter what I, or anyone else, said, he would do things only the way he wanted. Although he was on a similar footing as myself, he considered himself to be the most gifted leader in the department and acted as though he were its head.

I found myself terribly frustrated by his political maneuverings, and constant harangues on how things had to be done. I counted the days until my contract expired. It was a most unpleasant way to live.

It was at this point that I reread "The Invading Cat" and it was as if The Mouser herself were whispering in my ear. I realized that this colleague fit the passage to a tee. To my embarrassment, I also understood that I had allowed every one of his incursions!

The next time I saw him, I stood up to his bullying. I stated my views, told him that I would not be swayed, and that I had the backing of the true head of the department.

From then on, when I ran into the invading cat, I made sure to hold firm on anything that was important. I gave him some small victories – things that held no importance to me – but on everything else, I was resolute. Eventually, he learned that I was no longer allowing his encroachment, so he avoided me.

I had repelled the invading cat for good!

If you know a similar person in your life, it is time to take a stand. Allow him his small victories, because it's important not to swing too far in the other direction. The world turns on compromise. But with those things that are important, be intractable.

"He is trying to take what is not his: your thoughts and your territory." The Mouser knew that the really important things are not negotiable. Don't let anyone tell you what you must think or feel. Don't let anyone tell you that what is yours is now his. Resist the invading cat.

The Shame-filled Cat

"Some cats feel lacking to even the simplest hunting. These cats cannot shed their shame. If the shame-filled cat catches the mouse, he feels another would have caught it faster, easier, or with more [finesse]. If he loses the mouse, his hunger is a constant reminder of his failure. He lives in fear, burns with inadequacy, and hides from the pleasures of a blowing leaf or a jumping cricket. The shame-filled cat seeks barren territory, for he feels undeserving of sunny grasses and high perches. And when confronted he will relinquish even what little he has, his fear overwhelming. He will cower, his tail low, his claws sheathed, so certain that he will lose, he dare not try. To regain his rightful place, he must shed his shame as he does his coat in summer heat. He must rub it from his face and whiskers on the rough bark of pride. He must bury it, as he would his waste. Shame has no place in the mind of a cat. **"**

The message in "The Shame-filled Cat" is one that humans can easily understand. Many people live with debilitating shame. It's an emotion that can get its claws into the human psyche and is difficult to dislodge.

"The Shame-filled Cat" was a bit of a revelation for me, for I never thought of cats as creatures who dealt with shame. They always appear so confident and prideful. Yet even as I thought that, I realized the fallacy of the assumption. There are many people whom we look at and admire. We assume they are unacquainted with a negative self-image. But if you search behind their public façades, there can be many surprises. Perhaps the shame-filled cats are like these seemingly confident people who hide their inner demons.

Society puts great value on certain achievements, like success in business, raising obedient children, having money, etc. The definition of success may vary within different communities, but all strata have their ideals and goals. If you feel inadequate to the ideals of your community or its expectations, then you might experience some of the characteristics of the shame-filled cat. "If the shame-filled cat catches the mouse, he feels another

would have caught it faster, easier, or with more finesse." If you have shame issues, that statement probably feels familiar. A cat catching a mouse is, in their world, a success story. Yet instead of celebrating, the shame-filled cat finds ways to feel inadequate. This may seem counter-intuitive – why would success breed shame? It's because shame, with its insidious negativity, can make you feel undeserving.

"He lives in fear, burns with inadequacy, and hides from... pleasures..." speaks to this undeserving place inside of us that is firmly rooted in shame.

So what can you do to combat it? The Mouser gives you the answer in her uniquely feline way. "To regain his rightful place, he must shed his shame as he does his coat in summer heat. He must rub it from his face and whiskers on the rough bark of pride. He must bury it, as he would his waste."

Note how The Mouser immediately tries to draw in the reader with the metaphor of "shedding" shame. This would've been a clear image for her students. Humans may not think of themselves as shedders, but we are. We are forever sloughing off skin cells and shedding our hair. To be alive is to be forever changing. We get rid of that which no longer serves us and replace it with that which is fresh and healthy. So must we shed our shame.

To avoid being a shame-filled cat, means recognizing your own successes. It means feeling deserving of pleasure and good things in your life. It means valuing yourself.

Once you accept that you have value, then shame has no place in your soul. It will fall from your shoulders like a strand of hair pushed aside by new growth. Just as shame "has no place in the mind of a cat," it also has no place in the mind of a good, contributing member of the community like you.

The Catnip Cat

"Catnip is a gift from The Mother Creator to her kittens. It allows us to seek a higher energy, making our play keener and more determined. But to rely on catnip is to worship a false god. We are not our true self when under its spell. Some cats love the false keenness and cannot feel alive without it. They use it to hunt, to chase a string, to roll under a human's touch, and to give insincere strength when protecting their territory. When their catnip is gone, they care not about work, play, or affection. They seek only more catnip. In this way, catnip can kill and torture the addicted cat. Be wise in its use. For a few moment's pleasure, rub it on your face and kick it with your hind paws. Do not hunt under its fog. Do not court under its haze. Teach your kittens to nip with conscientiousness. **"**

At first glance, this story is a warning against the evils of addictive behavior and living under recreationally altered states. However, if you look closer, you'll see that it's really an admonition about excess. The Mouser does not tell her students to "just say no" to catnip. If its use is casual and controlled, she finds nothing wrong with it. It's only when a cat uses the drug to excess, allowing it to become more important than the necessities of life, that she warns against its use.

Saying no to illegal drugs isn't all that difficult for most people, but controlling urges around legal addictive substances is much more challenging. People use excessive drinking, eating, smoking, sex, or caffeine as balms for the emptiness they feel inside. Still others go on buying binges, spending money they don't have in order to surround themselves with meaningless material possessions.

Whatever your addiction, you must first recognize it, and then work toward controlling it. Whether you need to eliminate it completely (like smoking) or find new, healthier approaches (as toward eating), it is up to you to take charge of your own life. Stop allowing your addictions to control you, as catnip controls the feline in The Mouser's example.

It might seem impossible to change. It isn't. Addictions tend to be caused by buried hurts. Seek out the pain that you are feeding with your bad habit. Shine a harsh light upon it, and work toward freeing yourself of its grip. Once you do, you will probably no longer need the balm of alcohol, food, cigarettes, sex, or spending. There is no need to feed that which is not hungry. Eliminating the source of pain will free you from your addictive habits.

The Story of Mew Ling

As a kitten, Mew Ling was attacked by a large tom and left to die. However, she managed to survive and her wounds eventually healed, but the damage to her life was done. She was left with the feeling that to experience love or friendship was to welcome hurt and pain.

Wanting to be as far from the tom as possible, she went in search of new territory and eventually came to a great wall that stretched like the spine of a dragon as far as her eyes could see. She loved the wall, aspiring to build one as great and impregnable around her own heart. She followed its length, unsure if she would ever find its end even if she used all of her nine lives in which to search. She was very curious about what lay on the other side but alas, it was too tall to leap.

Finally, after many years and adventures, she came to the end of the wall. Yet when she looked beyond it, she saw only territory much like that on her side of the wall. There were no glorious fields filled with mice, or streams made of milk. Disappointed, she stretched on her back to take a quick nap.

When she awoke, a wandering tom was standing nearby. "My life has been wasted," he said. "For years I have traveled this wall, wanting to see what lay on your side, and I find that it is the same as mine."

Mew Ling realized that she and the tom had traveled parallel paths, both using their quest as an excuse not to love. Yet both had found only disappointment. Having been given a chance to change their fates, they brought forth a litter. They advised their kittens to search to their heart's desire, but to stay far away from walls. Walls only serve to confine your dreams. But if you do find it necessary to build a wall, always include a gate.

Yo Meow Ma predates the building of China's Great Wall by hundreds of years. So to what wall does she refer? Just as a wall around one's heart refers not to a physical barrier, but to a psychological one, so does the wall that Mew Ling traveled. What kept her confined was her own fear, not some man-made obstacle.

There might be times in your life when you might feel that safety and protection are worth far more than the benefits of risk. Perhaps you've been hurt by a former spouse, or, like Mew Ling, were abused as a child. A natural reaction to physical or emotional pain, is to avoid the circumstances that caused it in the first place.

But to live life without taking any chances, is to live timidly and alone. If you never gamble your heart, you risk losing the opportunity of reaping the rewards of true love, deep friendships, and honest relationships. The wall that Mew Ling and the tom admired so fervently was, in its way, their prison.

The Mouser is careful to note that the lesson both cats learned was that walls, whether real or around your heart, "only serve to confine your dreams." It is this realization that allows both cats to open themselves to a new future – one filled with companionship, children, love, and unconfined dreams.

You, too, can find the end of your walls, or at the very least, a gate. Walk through and you will see that the walls don't just keep others out, they also keep you in. Take the risk. Happiness flows toward the person most willing to allow it in.

A well-timed awkward pounce
is worth a dozen graceful,
empty, leaps.

The Spoiled Cat

"The spoiled cat wants, but does not need. She demands without work or favor. If you give to a spoiled cat, expect nothing, for she feels she deserves your gifts. Inside the spoiled cat is emptiness. She thinks that gifted mice, your bathing tongue, and lazy sleep will fill this emptiness. They cannot. The spoiled cat has difficulty seeing past the surfaces of her life. Do not mistake this blindness for hopelessness. The spoiled cat can be filled. If she looks inside and espies the dark void, she will find questions. When she gives freely to another without thought of reward, she will find answers. Do not feed the spoiled cat. Instead, ask her to feed you. Only this way, are you her provider."

Everyone likes to be pampered and spoiled at times, but if this is the only way you can convince yourself of your worth, then you resemble the spoiled cat. The Mouser outlines the pitfalls of this behavior – always getting and never giving – and they are recognizable even though her language is targeted to cats.

The heart of this passage lies not in her defining the spoiled cat, but with her insight into what is behind the behavior. She speaks of an internal void. It is this emptiness that all the surface pleasures try to fill. But no amount of gifts can fill those dark places you might find inside yourself.

"If she looks inside, espies the dark void, and recognizes her pain, she will find questions." The Mouser understands that the root of this behavior is pain – often an old and powerful hurt. To assuage that pain, you can do many things. If it was caused by an imbalance of power – like an abusive parent or spouse – then you might grow into the habit of exercising your power over another to prove that you, and not the abuser, are in charge. In the spoiled cat, that power manifests in a desire to make others do your bidding.

Another balm for the pain is to bury your hurt with a mountain of material objects, thinking that happiness and fulfillment can be bought instead of earned. These are the surfaces of life to which The Mouser refers. She knew that ownership of objects is never the path to filling internal emptiness.

Acquisition gives only a fleeting sense of happiness. When that joy fades, the pain returns. It is a never-ending cycle of selfish attaining and festering hurt.

To break the cycle, whether it is based on power or acquisition, is difficult, but worthwhile. It is important to face the source of your pain and diffuse it of its power over you. If you can rid yourself of the hurt, you can begin to fill your internal void with love, caring, and generosity. To give to another from your heart brings a satisfaction that is immeasurably deeper than you will ever get from a material possession.

But perhaps you are not spoiled, yet you know someone who is. Is there anything you can do? Wisely, Yo Meow Ma gives advice to the cats who live with or around a spoiled cat. If you have someone in your life who fits this profile, then you are probably weary of the imbalances in your relationship. Trying to find equality with someone who is forever demanding power or tributes can leave you wondering if it is worth having that person in your life.

With her statement, "Do not feed the spoiled cat. Instead, ask her to feed you. Only this way, are you her provider," The Mouser suggests that you turn the tables on your spoiled friend by trying to switch roles. Ask her to be the giver. She may try to evade or even outright refuse, but it's important that you remain loving but strong. If you succeed, you will provide your friend with something far more valuable than gifts or trinkets. Demanding equality in your relationship could bring about a journey of self-discovery for your friend.

One good purr deserves another.

_____

The Passionate Cat

"The passionate cat finds joy in every day of each of her nine lives. Whether great or small, each gift of the Mother Creator is celebrated in her heart. The passionate cat purrs her life's rhythms, instead of mewling at every imagined setback. She is not this way because her territory is larger, or her fur more groomed than other cats. Her passion comes from seeking buoyant moments, and finding them all around her. Sometimes, the passionate cat becomes a Mouser. The passionate Mouser creates a world where the things that enthuse her, can enthuse others. Unselfish, she shares her passion and her purring with as many cats as will listen. That they, too, will purr is in no doubt. **"**

This lesson is one of The Mouser's most important. It outlines an entire way of life. If you can live each day with the attitudes outlined here, you are all but guaranteed a life of happiness and fulfillment.

It does take work to achieve the level of appreciation for simple joys that Yo Meow Ma outlines. It means cultivating the ability to find the positives in every experience. That's easy to do when things are going right. But the real test is to continue to experience joy even when things aren't looking so bright.

Happily, The Mouser gives you the key to doing this. "Her passion comes from seeking buoyant moments, and finding them all around her." There is a wonderful sense of imagery in the phrase "seeking buoyant moments." We can almost see those positives floating to the top of a bad day, bobbing happily above all the negativity below them. Those buoyant moments are the key to your staying afloat. Hold them close to you; allow

them inside of you. Gather enough of them, and there will be no room left for negativity.

But what about when things go wrong? The Mouser answers that question with: "The passionate cat purrs her life's rhythms, instead of mewling at every imagined setback." It is important to examine the negatives to see if they are real or imagined. For example, what if you lose your job? You might see that as a major setback, with no joy to be found. And while you're in the midst of it, you might find it impossible to see it any other way. But perhaps in a year or so, you might look back and think that it was one of the best things that ever happened to you. Maybe you found a new, better job that you'd have never known about if you hadn't lost the old one. Or maybe you fell in love while searching for a new position. Or perhaps you decided to change the direction of your life and start a brand new career.

Sometimes, when you are in the midst of challenging times, it is very difficult to see the buoyant moments and the positive threads. But isn't it possible that you aren't seeing them because you aren't looking? What would happen if you consciously searched every negative moment for a positive aspect? Chances are, you would become a passionate cat.

Once you practice looking for simple joys in dreary or negative moments, you may even attain the next level: the passionate Mouser. In this enlightened state, you can affect not only yourself, but those around you.

Think of one thing in your life about which you feel passionate. It may be your job, a hobby, a talent, or a cause. Let's say that you love music, and adore writing songs, but don't know if anyone will like the songs you write. These questions don't stop you, though. You continue to write songs, infusing them with your love, passion, and energy. By pouring those positive pieces of yourself into your songwriting, the music you create has a real chance of touching the souls of others. Music isn't just notes played or sung in sequence. It can have a visceral, emotional effect on the listener. What you put into your songs can also come out – and therefore make the listener feel what you were feeling when you wrote them.

Everything you do can have this effect. If you are passionate, then that passion can be contagious. The more people you share your passion with, the more people will have their lives made more buoyant by you.

The Avoiding Cat

" *The avoiding cat plays games in her mind. If she needs to clean her fur, she hunts. If she needs to fill her belly, she sleeps. If she needs to explore her territory, she toys with a leaf. Her actions are often spirited, though misdirected. The avoiding cat is fear-filled. She has more comfort working with diligence on a different task, than facing her fear of the task at paw. If she fears she will hunt without success, she will do any other thing to avoid that failure. The longer she avoids, the more fear she builds, and the hungrier she will get. The hunger will weaken her, and that will increase her fear, keeping her evermore from the hunt. The avoiding cat is not weak, lazy, or inadequate. She is afraid. To help herself, she must face her fear and do her tasks anyway. This is effortless to say, but difficult to do. Yet she must, as only clawing at fear can diminish it.* **"**

Apparently, procrastination is as common to cats as it is to humans. Avoidance behavior is a difficult problem, as it can lead to some serious consequences.

There are many kinds of procrastination, many of which appear to have different causes. But in the end, as The Mouser tells us, it all boils down to fear. Whether you're a pleasure-seeking procrastinator, or a tension-filled self-doubter, the only way to amend your behavior is to recognize what fear is driving it, and then by facing that fear to dispel it.

If you are an avoiding cat, you are "not weak, lazy, or inadequate." You might spend a lot of energy accusing yourself of having one, two, or all three of these attributes. That kind of negative self-talk can stand between you and the underlying fear that you're trying to discover.

Instead of calling yourself names, or mentally berating yourself, try to figure out what fear is at the heart of your behavior. Are you like the cat who feels inadequate to the task, and therefore doesn't try? Or do you hold impossibly high standards for yourself, and because they are unattainable, you avoid trying and therefore avoid the inevitable failure? Do you fear success? After all, success could change many aspects of your life. Perhaps you think it's better to avoid a task that might bring success, so that you don't have to deal with a changed life.

It's possible that you fear losing control. If someone in authority demands that you do something, and you do whatever you can to avoid the task, you might be in a struggle for control. "No one can make me do what I don't want to," you might think, even if not doing the task hurts you far more than doing it would have.

The Story of Qi Tan and Qi Tee

Qi Tan and Qi Tee were littermates. Even as a kitten, Tan excelled in pouncing. His mother was filled with pride and forecast that he would some day be a great hunter. Tee, however, struggled with her pouncing. It did not come naturally, so Tee had to spend many hours of every day practicing. Her mother worried that she would never see the second of her nine lives.

After they had weaned, and gained enough age, they found their own territories. Their land shared a common border yet they rarely crossed paths. Tan was such a splendid hunter, he spent most of his days sleeping and playing, because he knew that it would take little effort to capture prey. Tee worked hard, toiling with relentless will to improve her skills.

One day, they were both patrolling their shared border, and saw the other as if anew. Tee was shocked at Tan's bony frame. She asked him why he did not eat his fill, for the area was bountiful with rodents and birds. Tan told her that he had spent so much time playing and sleeping that his talent had withered and died. Since he had never learned any hunting skills, and had relied solely on his talent, he was unable to feed himself. He could only watch as mice teased his tail, and birds plucked at the tips of his ears.

Tee quickly captured a stout and wily rat, and brought it to him. Tan was stunned at her ability, when as a kitten she had so lacked in any talent. Tee had not spent her days sleeping and playing. She had worked every day on her hunting and through practice and dedication had become a master hunter. Humbled, Tan asked that she teach him the skills, and she agreed. With her help, and much practice and dedication, Tan became a hunter once again. Both lived through many summers, and died fat.

The Story of Qi Tan and Qi Tee juxtaposes Tan's innate talents against his sister's worth ethic. Both Tan and Tee have the potential of being great hunters, though it is obvious in Tan's case, and unknowable in Tee's.

Tan teaches us that skills and talents, if allowed to lie fallow, can disappear. And Tee teaches us that hard work and perseverance can overcome the hand genetics deals you.

It's a simple message, but told with great affection. It is obvious that Tan and Tee care for each other. When Tee discovers that Tan is in trouble she immediately pounces into action to help her brother. And when Tan sees this, he admires what his sister has achieved and asks for her help. Not all families are as supportive of one another, though I think it's fair to say, most people would wish that they were.

It's possible that the underlying story of familial love carries as strong, or stronger, a message as the more overt parable about using talents and working hard. Close family bonds, love, support, encouragement, recognition – Tan and Tee have much to teach us.

When standing on sand, bury
your waste, not your head.

The Greedy Cat

"Some cats want more than their share. The greedy cat wants the biggest territory and covets the mice and birds that escape his borders. He gives no thought to the hunger of others, or his own sated belly. He must have everything. When he mates, he kills the kittens of his mate, for all kittens must come from him. When he feeds, he eats every part, leaving nothing for the scavengers. It makes him ill, but he cares more about having everything than he does for his own health. The greedy cat doesn't understand that having more territory and more mice does not equal having more friends and mates. The greedy cat is impoverished, in this sense. And when the greedy cat dies, the scavengers, once denied, eat their fill. He does not receive the sorrow of other cats. His territory, his mice, birds, fishes, rats, and pika are no longer his. The greedy cat lives to have everything, but dies with nothing. "

J have a confession to make. Sometimes I fear that I am the greedy cat, because I desperately want to know everything there is to learn about Yo Meow Ma. I am never satisfied, and at times, I am even envious of the discoveries made by my colleagues.

I make this confession because it's important to remember that greed is not synonymous with money. Greed can take many forms, but in its essence, it is about wanting to have more than others, or more than we need. I don't need to know everything about Yo Meow Ma in order to learn from her, just as the greedy cat doesn't need to possess every mouse and pika.

We live in a world of excess. Material possessions take on exaggerated importance in order to make us feel successful. In the academic world, the measure of "wealth" is knowledge.

You may have something that you're chasing, as well. It might be money, but it can also be something else. Think about your life, and consider those things for which you demonstrate greed. How is your quest impacting your life? The Mouser tells us that the greedy cat is impoverished because he has no friends or family. He has only territory and food, which might be a measure of wealth in the cat world, but is not a measure of any being's spirit.

In "The greedy cat lives to have everything, but dies with nothing," The Mouser sums up the basic flaw with any greedy pursuit. In the end, the measure of a soul is not in what was possessed, but in what was contributed. If you give back to the world some of what you've taken, then greed can be neutralized. You won't die with nothing if the end of your life shows a tapestry of friends, family, contributions to society, and helpful deeds.

The book you're holding is due in part to my having read "The Greedy Cat." It made me think about my own life, and my single-minded pursuit of knowledge about Yo Meow Ma. I wanted to share that knowledge with others. The result of this decision is that I have found a level of joy in the sharing that I'd never achieved in the narrow world of accruing facts. Across the span of thousands of years, a cat has made me realize the worth of my own life.

If you have greed inside of you, examine it, and ask yourself if it is serving you. I'm not advocating a life of total self-denial. There is nothing wrong with being wealthy, or having a lot of knowledge, or owning a host of possessions. I'm simply asking you to look at your life to see if there is an imbalance. Do you have more greed than compassion? Are your possessions or money more important to you than the people who love you? Is there something you can do, right now, that could offset this imbalance?

The greedy cat died alone and un-mourned. His territory went to other cats, his mice fed other bellies, and the world kept on spinning. You have one chance to make an impact on the world. Use your compassion and generosity to fight whatever greed lies within, and make your impact a positive one.

You have as much power over the movements of a mouse as you have over the direction of the wind. Do not destroy your happiness over what you cannot control.

The Heroic Cat

"It is said that to find eternity, a cat must be heroic. The heroic cat cares for others as she cares for herself. She treats other cats with respect and kindness. Some think heroism is defined by courageous deeds. It can be. But it is also in a life well lived. The heroic cat will hunt for you when you are sick or injured. She will protect your kittens when you are using the sand. She will share her den if you are caught in cold winds. She will groom you, and make you purr. The heroic cat does not trespass on your territory, leave scent in your spaces, or hunt your creatures. The heroic cat is she whom every cat should long to be. "

The Mouser's descriptions of heroic acts, rooted in the wonderfully mundane, shows a sophistication of thought that still has the power to surprise me. Ask a human child what a hero is, and he will most likely answer superheroes, fire fighters, or policemen. Yet this ancient cat knew that those who do obviously courageous deeds are not the only ones who fit that title.

There are heroes all around you, if you'll look beyond stereotypes and notice the kind of everyday courage it takes to live a good and giving life. Heroes can be the man who gives a percentage of his salary to charity, the woman who volunteers to sign in blood donors, the teacher who spends some precious minutes with a troubled student even though it's time to go home, or the person who looks at you from the mirror every morning.

Every time you are honest, even though a lie would be much easier, you are a hero. Whenever you hold open a door for a stranger, yield to a merging vehicle on a busy street, or give your spare change to someone down on his luck, you become someone else's momentary hero. There are as many ways to be heroic as there are to be kind.

This is not to cheapen the sort of deeds we usually consider to be heroic. There are people in this world who have earned the moniker a thousand times over. But those are the examples that are bold, bright, and obvious. The small heroic moments in a less extraordinary lifestyle also need to receive their due. If more people saw the greatness in ordinary people, perhaps they would strive to become heroic as well. Imagine a world filled with people whose primary goal was to be kind to others. It would change everyone's life in a fundamental way.

The Holding Cat

"The holding cat has difficulty letting go. When summer approaches, he does not shed. He holds on to his winter coat, his appearance disheveled and unkempt. The heat of his unshed fur makes him clumsy and artless when he hunts. He sleeps fitfully, too warm to find release. His territory resembles his coat, with bits of bone, fur, and feathers around his den. His trails are overgrown and slow him when he runs. The holding cat clings to things that do not serve him. He may think this keeps him safe, for other cats rarely invade the territory of a holding cat. But when it is time to mate, the females do not answer his call. They do not want his messy coat near their gleaming fur. In this way, the holding cat hides from the rest of the world, never demanding of himself his obligations to the community. The things he hoards have little meaning. The fur that covers him gives little pleasure. The holding cat holds only illusions. "

It's easy to fall into the patterns of a holding cat. You might fill your living space with clutter, or hold onto extra weight, or keep people in your life who no longer serve you. If you tend to hold onto things, you may have difficulty letting them go. You may even be blind to much of what you keep, not seeing the clutter in your home, or ignoring the extra pounds.

Many people who hold onto unnecessary things see them as a kind of protection. After all, if your home is too cluttered, you can't entertain guests. This keeps you from having to interact with the outside world, or risking a new relationship. But is this what you truly desire? Is isolation a healthy goal?

You might have the opposite problem. Some people clutter their lives with all sorts of people so that they never have to become too close with any one person. Both behaviors – whether cluttering your environment to keep people out, or cluttering your social life to keep close relationships at bay – are symptoms of a fear of intimacy.

This fear is also responsible for many of the weight problems people have. By putting a wall around yourself, in this case a wall of flesh, you can protect yourself from having to become too intimate with anyone.

All of these holding behaviors have their purpose. It's up to you to ask yourself if that purpose is what you want in your life.

Is it more important to hold onto thousands of cluttering "things" that you don't use or care about, or to open your life to new people and experiences? Is it more important to hold onto extra pounds that slow you down and endanger your life, or to allow yourself to get close to someone special?

Personally, I find that I often fit the pattern of the holding cat. I have tried to change my ways, but it's difficult. When I find myself struggling with it, I remember The Mouser's words: "The holding cat holds only illusions." I find it helpful to see my problems in this area as mere illusions. It's the illusion of safety (keeping out people who could hurt you), or the illusion of wealth (owning lots of things), or the illusion of independence (holding onto excess weight or claiming you have no one special in your life because you value your independence), or many other illusions for which we cover our own inadequacies.

You may also be holding onto emotional clutter. Perhaps you were hurt in childhood by an abuser, and have held onto that hurt your entire life. As difficult as it is to have such a damaging experience, it's far worse to hold that experience inside you like a raw wound. It can become an excuse for bad behavior, the reason you cite for failure, or the millstone you hang from your neck to keep you from achieving.

What the abuser did was wrong, but what you might be doing to yourself can be far worse. What benefit do you receive from holding onto that hurt, digging constantly into that wound, and nurturing the pain instead of the healing? Holding onto emotional hurt makes you take on the role of abuser. At some point, you will have to release your hold on the pain, in order to heal.

It's time to let go. Don't hold onto illusions or the things that represent them. Free yourself of any cluttered area in your life, whether it's physical clutter or emotional clutter. Only then will you cleanse your soul of the holding cat.

The Story of Pu S'se and Pu Ma

Pu S'se loved to hunt, and would often discuss her kills with her littermates. S'se caught many furred prey, including a corpulent rat that fed her for three full days. The other cats gave much adoration to her for her skills. S'se's littermate, Pu Ma, was also skilled. Ma had a taste for feathered food, and concentrated her efforts on chasing birds. S'se, who was acknowledged as the finest hunter in her province, applauded Ma's efforts. But inside her heart, she felt Ma was foolish to chase such difficult prey. What did barren chases get you? Nothing but more hunger.

During mating season, the toms wandered through the province, crying for a mate. S'se knew she was the most admired, due to her skills. But this year, the toms did not come as expected. Only one cried her name and he was small and bony, with fur that was dull and spotty — a hunter so poor, he could not be expected to feed her while she was heavy with kittens.

Angrily, S'se went searching for the vanished toms. Which cat was attracting all of the well-fed toms with shiny coats and healthy girth? In the distance, she heard a great meowling scream. It was the voice of heat, and S'se knew that she was near a female crying for a mate. To S'se's surprise, she heard dozens of answers, the voices strong and arrogant. This was where the toms were! But who was this cat who commanded such devoted attention?

It was Pu Ma! S'se could not believe it. Though attractive and clever, Ma had never before been first chosen by the toms. What had changed?

As she drew near, S'se noticed a curious pile of feathers near Ma's den. Ma saw her then and motioned her near. "Isn't it wonderful?" she asked, her whiskers quivering, her eyes sparkling. "I had no idea how many toms enjoy a meal with wings." S'se, who had been praised many times by Ma for her hunting skills, did not show her littermate the same regard. She made sport of Ma for eating scrawny, flying vermin, instead of stout and delicious mice and rats. She insulted the toms for their attention and returned to her territory in a cloud of selfish ire.

That year, S'se mated with the scrawny tom, because he remained the only cat who returned her howls. S'se's litter came early and all the kittens were sickly and died within days of their birth. Humbled by her own foolishness, she returned to Pu Ma's den, which now harbored a healthy litter of eight mewling kittens.

"I allowed envy to guide my voice," S'se said. "I saw your success as my failure. I have never caught a bird, and yet you have slain so many. You deserve the strongest tom and eight fat kittens. I deserve only starvation."

"No, dear sister," said Ma. "You are a far better hunter than any other when seeking warm fur. We both have success, and should only be enhanced by the kills of the other." She gifted S'se with a fat chick from a white crane. S'se ate the tender meat then made a bed of the downy feathers. Although the taste was quite pleasing, S'se continued to hunt only those with fur. Her success continued, but she no longer felt herself better than other hunters. Pu S'se grew to old age well-fed, well-mated, and with many generations at her paws.

This delicious tale of sibling rivalry, envy, and competition is another story that is found throughout the cat world. The only change of note is that cats who live near the sea talk of Pu Ma's skill as a fishing cat, instead of a birding cat. The basic lesson, however, remains the same.

Pu S'se is rejected by the toms not because she had suddenly failed in her hunting –from what is written, she remained a skilled rat-catcher – but because she derided the toms – evidenced by the fact that they had been seeking her out in years past. It isn't clear why they stopped coming *en masse* (with the exception of the scrawny tom), but one has to assume the jibes and insults became too much. Human beings have arrogantly proclaimed themselves the superiors of the animal kingdom for many millennia. It's time that we amend that short-sighted view. We can no longer assume that the animals who share our planet don't have the same feelings, foibles, motivations, thoughts, and moral quandaries as we do.

If it does nothing else, the work of Yo Meow Ma shines a light onto that erroneous point of view. In a way, humans have been the Pu S'ses of the world – shouting about our superior ways and deriding those who don't reach our exalted standards. If we don't change our ways, we will end up like that misguided cat in the year of the scrawny tom – alone and unloved.

This same warning can be used in any aspect of your life. It's easy to become envious of someone who appears to have more success than you. Or to feel superior to one who has less. Neither position is healthy for your spirit. It's always a better choice to celebrate the success of others, especially those who you love or care for. If your friend receives a promotion and you do not, remember what Pu S'se said upon her awakening: "I saw your success as my failure." Your friend's success is not your failure. It is simply her success.

A little healthy competition can be fun and necessary. It can often spur you to greater achievements. But not everything is a competition. And not every contest needs to be won. Pick only those that serve your higher good, and leave the rest out of your heart. It's okay to compete as long as you are not projecting your self worth onto the outcome.

Pu S'se and Pu Ma learned to share the toms, each concentrating on her food of choice. By sticking to what they did best, they did not have to compete for food. That's a greater legacy than any amount of mice or birds could give. Let your dreams rise above petty competitions and perhaps you, too, will find a higher purpose.

Live each of your nine lives as if
you have only one.

The Winged Cat

"It is the destiny of all cats to seek closeness with the sky. Only from great heights can you see your territory with its potential dangers and succulent meals. Many ask, why were we not born with wings? You have them. As the birds wing on sky and the fish wing on water, cats wing on land. You leap great heights – is this not winged? You fall and are not crushed – is this not winged? You are faster than your prey – is this not winged? The winged cat knows he needs not feathers to fly. Claw up a towering tree and you are part of the sky. From this height you see as a bird can. What need have you for feathers? The winged cat does not long for what is not his. He takes his own gifts and makes them enough."

The appeal of this passage isn't difficult to understand. To a cat, it probably feels like a motivational speech – stirring and energizing. Even I was moved, and for a moment, wished that I were a winged cat.

Upon reflection, I realized that we all have the potential to be winged. Each of us has talents and skills that can be elevating; these can be our wings.

What you should aspire to be is the best possible human being that it is within your power to be. To do this, you must use those talents and skills with which you were born. This doesn't mean that if you have a good singing voice you have to quit your job and become a professional singer. It simply means that you find time in your life to sing. Whether it's with a church choir, lullabies for your children, or in your shower, allow your voice its release. Nothing ever has to come of it – you don't have to make everything in your life be about success, fortune, and competition. But to use a talent is to revel in the joy of it. Make that your goal and everything else is a bonus.

You also can adapt talents. For example, you might have an ear for mimicry. Perhaps you can imitate the voices of celebrities. With a refined ear for human speech you might find yourself able to write dialogue and use this talent to write a play, film, or novel. Only you know what your talents and skills are. Use them, nurture them, adapt them – just be certain you don't allow them to lie fallow.

The other important message The Mouser gives us is to live without envy. "The winged cat does not long for what is not his." Just as it is useless for a cat to wish for wings, so is it an exercise in frustration for you to long for gifts you do not have. Instead of yearning for the impossible, make what is already yours into a source of infinite joy. If you can't sing, perhaps you could learn an instrument. If you can't play sports, perhaps you could referee.

The possibilities are endless. If you have an interest, but no talent in that area, find another way to get involved. If you have a talent, but no way to incorporate it into the mainstream of your life, allow it into the margins. There's no reason to cry for wings when you already have all the gifts you'll ever need.

The sheathed claw wins
no battles.

_____

The Aspiring Cat

"The aspiring cat wants more than an ordinary life. When others hunt mice, she hunts rats. When others settle for nesting chicks, she hunts birds on the wing. When others are pleased with a fish washed onto shore, she immerses herself in the stream. The aspiring cat dreams for her kittens, as well as herself. She teaches them to desire for themselves. The aspiring cat is rare. Most cats are content to fill their bellies, create litters, and defend their territories. But the aspiring cat wants more. She does not do these things out of greed or to humble those around her. It is a need deep within her heart. She is true to herself when she shows her ambitions. Her dreams can take many forms. She can be the best hunter, the most nurturing mother, the most popular mate, the greatest climber, the most diligent protector, or the wisest Mouser. If you are an aspiring cat, do not fight your dreams. **"**

It is never easy to have high goals, big dreams, or far-flung ambitions. It's difficult for you and for those who love you. These higher aspirations can lead to a life with very little security, filled with pitfalls and rejection, or isolation.

But if you've decided to follow that unbeaten path, you know that an ordinary life isn't for you. You were born to reach farther, and so you do, regardless of the consequences.

Not everyone with big dreams is reaching for the stars. There are many steps along the way, and each can carry risk. If you want to be an actress, you can try to be a superstar, or try to land roles at the local repertory theatre. If you want to play sports you can try to win a gold medal at the Olympics or play for an intramural team. If you want to go into business, you can try to be CEO of a major corporation, or try for a position in management.

For aspiring cats, the goal is always the highest they can go. Ask yourself if you aspire, or are you content with smaller goals? If you aspire to the greatest heights your talents and skills can take you, then allow The Mouser's words inside of you, as comfort when things grow difficult.

"She does not do these things out of greed or to humble those around her. It is a need deep within her heart. She is true to herself when she shows her ambitions." This is the essence of aspiration. It is indeed a need deep inside of you. It can be difficult to explain to others, and can take its toll as you strive. But to deny this need is to deny your spirit. Take comfort in your own certainty that you were born to live a life beyond the ordinary.

The Sleepless Cat

❝Sleep is one of our greatest gifts. But the sleepless cat thinks that he is special. He robs himself of many naps, thinking that he is stronger, and less needful than others. In this way, he shows that he is not mindful of his health. The sleepless cat thinks himself impervious to the harm of stolen rest. He does not see the spiral into which he falls. To sleep less, he needs more energy. To build more energy, he needs more meals. To hunt more meals, he needs more sleep. Without sleep, his mind is not sharp, his body is depleted, and his energy is lacking. The sleepless cat can stop this spiral with self-care. Predators are chosen creatures, gifted with sleep as a reward for their skills. There is no predator as great as the cat. Therefore, sleep is nature's way of taking care of her most valuable creatures. **❞**

Cats sleep 16-18 hours a day while humans need only an average of 6-8 hours of sleep per night. But the difference in species' requirement doesn't lessen the impact of The Mouser's words. Without a proper amount of sleep, you will have as much difficulty as the sleepless cat.

Your body needs to rejuvenate itself, and it does so in the deepest stages of sleep. With so much to do, and so little time in which to do it, you may find it a simple choice to steal some extra work hours from your sleep time. You may think you don't need to rest for so long. That time would be better spent working, doing chores, or winding down from a difficult day. But the toll this "theft" will take on your health carries a heavy price.

Like a battery that needs recharging, your mind and body crave the deepest form of sleep. During this part of the night, your heart and lungs slow perceptibly, and your mind is resting at nearly coma levels. In this stage you slowly build the energy to face a new day.

Dreaming is also important. You may not remember your dreams, but they occur every night. They are your mind's way of processing the day, and sending messages between your conscious and subconscious mind. They can be a release for stress, a way to find hidden solutions to problems, or a relaxing flight of fantasy. Your mind needs dreams to stay healthy.

The Mouser knew that a cat's health was directly tied to the amount of sleep he got. As predators, cats were made to live with short bursts of energy and long periods of rest. Humans face similar challenges, needing energy to drive us through our day, and sleep to recharge us through the night. Don't steal those extra hours from the very thing that gives you the health to live your waking life.

The Story of Hao Ska't

Hao Ska't was born of humble circumstances, yet felt herself superior to her birth and her ancestors. Not wanting other cats to see her true station, she invented tales of importance. Other cats believed these tales, for to be untruthful is not our way. Ska't was so pleased with the effect of her falsehoods that she found other excuses to invent many more. Soon she had weaved the lies so firmly into her life that dishonesty was more comfortable for her than candor.

She built stories of adventures, hunts, and matings that made her appear a most desirable cat. She changed territories frequently, becoming the center of attention among the simple cats of each new home. But always, her lies crossed and twisted until even her most firm believers found only doubt. Although she had five summers, she had never borne kittens. Most cats would be saddened by this, but not Ska't. What she did not have, she invented. In yet another province, she boasted about the generations she had brought forth. The toms vied for her attention, thinking she would be a loving mother to their litters. But Ska't was too selfish to share her life with anyone, even the product of her womb. Leaving a trail of shattered hearts and withered lies, Ska't disappeared again.

The story of Hao Ska't spread. No matter where she went, she was always known. She was called a scoundrel and vilified throughout the middle kingdom. No tom would mate, no territory went undefended, no cat would groom or welcome her. Alone and despised, Hao Ska't ran afoul of a bear while she was chasing a pika. The bear ate Ska't then died, poisoned by all the lies in her heart. This is why we call dishonest cats a "skat."

The story of Hao Ska't may be an exaggerated morality tale, designed to show the evils of lying. Ska't is a most reprehensible creature – narcissistic, uncaring, and a pathological liar – who swoops into areas filled with "simple cats" and destroys their trust.

In human society, there are people who behave like this. They find lies easier than the truth, and often get entangled in an outrageous web of half-truths, deceit, lies, and prevarication – none of which will they recant. It is astonishing to watch one of these personalities swear with conviction that his lie is the truth, even when the evidence to the contrary is so powerful that a child could see it.

You may have used lies to get yourself out of difficult situations, to keep from being untactful, or to cover for a minor transgression. "Little white lies" are common and carry few consequences if you're caught. But it's not difficult to blur the lines between "little white lies" and their more serious siblings. Once you start lying about something, it becomes very difficult to stop, as one falsehood begets another.

Honesty, regardless of how painful it might be, is almost always the better choice. This doesn't mean telling someone he or she is ugly, or denigrating someone's work. You can be tactful and still be honest. What it means is living with the truth of your actions and taking responsibility for them. It means living by a code of honor that prevents you from telling that very first lie that would inevitably lead to others. In short, don't allow yourself to become a skat.

The bigger the litter, the more need for a sitter.

The Patient Cat

"The greatest hunters are the most patient hunters. They do not pounce when first they spy their prey. They stalk, and hide, and wait until the moment when success can be achieved. The patient cat excels in other areas of her life as well. When heat comes, she does not accept the first tom who yowls. She chooses carefully, knowing that her kittens will have a greater chance to thrive if sired by a strong, successful father. The patient cat is alert to her world, thinking through the difficulties, watching for predators and prey, guarding her litters, and always aware that there is a time for everything, and that time is not always now. Be at one with time, and you can be a patient cat."

No one enjoys endless waiting. It makes you feel stuck or frozen in time. What The Mouser is advocating here is not a lifetime of patience without achievement. She is talking about the kind of patience that you control – the kind of patience you can incorporate into your life. If you are stalking opportunity, getting the timing just right could easily be the difference between getting what you want, or missing out completely. As The Mouser says, "...there is a time for everything, and that time is not always now." The trick is to figure out exactly what time is the correct one.

The more you work at patience, the more you will become attuned to time. Impatience is an uncomfortable state. It is often tense and stressful. Time seems to stretch because of this discomfort. It can quickly become unbearable.

Your decision to be patient is a decision to treat the passage of time without stress. It doesn't mean you have to waste your life waiting for something to happen. It doesn't mean you should sit passively, never acting. It means that you don't allow the natural progression of time to be a source of irritation. If you know that something takes three days, you don't spend those days wondering why it hasn't already happened. Instead spend the time focusing on something else. If three days pass and there's still no sign of it, then you can pursue the reason for the delay. This way, you will start your pursuit fresh, without three days of mental stress coloring your actions.

"Be at one with time, and you can be a patient cat," means time is something you can control only by your own attitude toward it.

The Fish-bound Cat

❝The fish-bound cat is willing to do that which is unpleasant, to reap wondrous rewards. Water is delicious to drink, but uncomfortable on the fur. When most of us are wetted, we vigorously groom until every trace of it is gone. The fish-bound cat willingly leaps into the stream, for he craves the taste of fish more than he fears the touch of water. There will be many times in your life when you will be faced with unpleasant tasks. It is a measure of your character if you can be like the fish-bound cat. Do what you must, endure the disagreeable, and reap the rewards of your stalwart will. ❞

The Fish-bound Cat and The Bird-bound Cat both speak of striving for higher goals but with a difference. The Fish-bound cat urges you to strive for great things even if they are difficult or unpleasant.

You can probably think of several things in your life that you do which have unpleasant tasks attached to good rewards. You may not, for example, enjoy washing the dishes or dusting, but the reward – a clean house – is worth it to you. Or, perhaps something much grander occurred to you. Large goals often include doings things you may not enjoy. But again, if the goal is something you really want, then it's worth it to slog through whatever difficult steps need to be taken, in order to achieve your heart's desire.

The clearest example would be childbirth. Women have to face nine months of a changing body, with many uncomfortable side effects. And after suffering through all that, they are faced with a terribly painful ordeal in order to give birth. But the reward is so miraculously wonderful that all of those complaints fade into nothingness at the first sight of the newborn child.

Like the fish-bound cat, there will be many times in your life when you are faced with an uncomfortable journey that ends in a good reward. You must ask yourself if the reward is worth it to you. If not, you will feel cheated at the end, and will regret your decision. But if it is, chances are the ordeal you endure will quickly fade to a memory in light of your achievement.

Whatever you have a taste for in your life, you'll find that the feeling of satisfaction you get can be directly proportional to what you had to do to get it. Although rewards are sweet, sometimes it is the journey that is the true nectar.

The Creative Cat

"Instinct guides many of our actions, but were instinct all there was, would we not all be the same? You are different than your littermates, your parents, your mates, and your friends. Every cat has her own way of living in this world. The creative cat innovates and discovers. She knows that within herself are thoughts that have not been formed by others. We are all creative cats in some ways. Do not mothers create litters? Do not toms create readiness in the mother? Do not kittens create mischief? Do not Mousers create questions? To be a creative cat, you need only see your world in different ways. Stalking and pouncing need not be the only way to hunt. Licking need not be the only way to groom. When you see that you limit yourself only to what has always been done, you can begin on the path to becoming a creative cat."

Creativity is a difficult subject to categorize, as it takes in such a wide spectrum of experiences. The Mouser introduces it first as individuality in the notion: "You are different than your littermates, your parents, your mates, and your friends." When that concept is understood, she adds the dimension of seeing things not as they are or always have been, but in a new and innovative way. "To be a creative cat, you need only see your world in different ways," is a wonderfully succinct way of telling all individuals that they are capable of creativity.

I've met people who claim that they have no creativity. But, after being with them for any period of time, I realize that they are seeing through a very narrow lens, i.e. they are not seeing their own "different ways" because their definition of creativity is too limited. Creativity isn't confined to overt areas like art, music, and literature. It can be found in every aspect of life. Yo Meow Ma uses the examples of hunting and grooming – hardly traditional outlets for creativity in the human world. Yet for a cat, those activities are of primary importance. One can only guess at some of the creative ways The Mouser's students began to hunt and groom after hearing this lesson!

Your own parallels to hunting and grooming can be anything. There are creative ways to do every job on earth. And when faced with problems, you are often called upon to come up with creative solutions.

How do you suddenly believe in yourself when you've lived your life thinking you were not born with creativity? It sounds too easy, but the answer

is to simply tell yourself you are, and then you will be. That is the first step you must take. If you say it often enough, you will begin to believe. You must also open your eyes to the inventive moments of your day. "Every cat has her own way of living in this world." You have your own way of living in this world, too.

You can begin, as The Mouser recommends, with your thoughts. "She knows that within herself are thoughts that have not been formed by others." Every time you think something that you have never heard before, you are creating. From your thoughts, move to your actions. Every time you solve a problem, you are creating. Move back and forth between your thoughts and your actions, noticing each time that you exhibit creativity, and soon you will not be able to convince anyone – especially yourself – that you are not a creative cat.

But perhaps you are one of those people who knows that you are creative. You may even live deep within your imagination every

day in a traditionally creative field. If so, you have probably experienced moments when you doubt yourself. Writer's block, for example, is an easy doorway to self-doubt. You may have felt as though all the creativity you ever possessed had somehow been leached from you.

If this describes you, there are many excellent methods of opening those closed-off floodgates. But the first step will always be the same – remind yourself that you are creative. Just as those who think they are non-creative, you must begin with positive affirmation of your gifts. It should be easier for you simply because your life is filled with the truth of this thought.

The Mouser sums up her lesson with a simple, elegant statement that is the basis for most creativity: "When you see that you need not limit yourself to what has always been, you can begin on the path to becoming a creative cat." Remove your limits; think outside of the ordinary, and you will be well on your way to becoming a creative cat.

The Angry Cat

"Some cats stalk through their lives as if under a dark, rain-filled cloud. They are not comfortable unless they are filled with rage. The angry cat never feels the warmth of the sun; he feels only the cool of the shade. He does not delight in the plump flesh of the mouse, he complains about the bones and fur. The angry cat fumes over the injustices in the world, but is rarely moved to right the wrongs. If he did, he would lose his anger, and that would leave him facing the frightening source of his rage. Beneath his anger is often hurt and fear. All cats are angry at some time in their lives. But the angry cat is that way at all times in his life. If you are an angry cat, look inside your heart and confront the hurt that causes your fury. When you do, you'll feel the warmth of the sun, and taste the succulence of the mouse."

The opening image of a cat stalking across a flaming landscape really sets the tone for this lesson. Using a series of images, The Mouser paints the picture of anger, unrest, and dissatisfaction. Nothing is right with the world and everything, regardless of how positive it appears, is a source of rage to the angry cat.

If you react to life's setbacks in a similar manner, you would do well to ask yourself why. While you are examining your emotions and motivations, you should also ask why you are more comfortable feeling the volatile sting of anger, than other, more peaceful emotions.

The Mouser's response to the latter is an examination of the source of anger. "The angry cat fumes over the injustices in the world, but is rarely moved to right the wrongs. If he did, he would lose his anger, and that would leave him facing the frightening source of his rage." And what is the source of your rage?

Most people, when asked that question, will name a specific person or event. "She lied to my friends and that really gets me mad" or "The

politicians are all crooked. I can't trust any of them, and it really irks me that they don't care about the welfare of their constituents!" There are countless reasons to get angry, from petty disagreements to deeply troubling issues. But at the heart of your anger is something else.

"Beneath his anger is hurt and fear." Anger is almost always tied to these two emotions. Being angry allows you to pretend that solutions can be found outside yourself, and are therefore out of your hands. Yet even if the surface problem is solved, your anger still remains. It might shift to another source, or smolder inside of you, but unless you deal with your own hurt and fear – the things that caused the anger in the first place – you will never escape the trap of being an angry cat.

Anger can alert you to problems, but it doesn't solve them. It tends to hold you frozen in its grip, frustrated and seething. The Mouser knew that the only way to truly dispel anger is to face those underlying emotions. Once you do that, you can work toward a solution, like dealing with the lying friend, or working to unseat the bad politician. That won't happen if you walk around with fire under your feet. Face your fear and acknowledge your hurt. Only then can you douse those flames and deal with life's setbacks with a rational and keen mind. At that point, it's up to you whether or not you want to taste a mouse!

The Enlightened Cat

"You can live your life in ordinary ways. You will exist – you will eat and sleep and mate and die – and never quest for more. There is nothing wrong with this, as it is your choice to make. But some cats will embark on a journey. They do not have to travel a wall, like Mew Ling, or even wander from their territory. Journeys can take many forms. The enlightened cat sees the world and all other cats as her teachers, and she learns from each. She discovers the prized role of questions and the ephemeral role of answers. She asks, and seeks, and quests, and maybe, if she is open enough, she walks the path to enlightenment. If she reaches this state, she can let it all go – teaching as she was taught, divining new questions, and creating new journeys for those who sit avid in her shadow. The enlightened cat is a Mouser. You have the potential to be a Mouser, if that is the path you seek. This is the journey I have made, and I invite you now to follow. **"**

One can almost imagine The Mouser's students listening to this lesson and dreaming of one day having the sagacity of their teacher. I know that as much as I have learned from the wisdom of Yo Meow Ma, I am still far from being enlightened.

Some of the world's religions, in particular Buddhism, include the concept of enlightenment. It is remarkable to me that a cat could not only have conceived of something so complex, but that she could also attain it.

The Mouser does not mention the elimination of desire and suffering, as Buddha taught, but rather focuses on the role of the Mouser as teacher. Perhaps it was too difficult to include everything an enlightened cat would experience in one lesson.

The Mouser begins this lesson by speaking of the ordinary. As always, she does not judge those who live unenlightened lives. She is as accepting of them as she is of those who seek more.

The Mouser instructs her students to learn from everyone they meet, asking questions and searching for answers. It is a marvelous way to think about your life, knowing that every experience, good and bad, is there to teach you. It requires some self-examination, as you may need to ask yourself some difficult questions in order to find the elusive answers. It is especially difficult when dealing with negative experiences. It often seems impossible to understand why some bad things happen, while the events are still fresh. But a bit of distance can sometimes give the events clarity.

If you become ill, you may rail at the fates for causing such a terrible thing. Yet later, you may find yourself embracing life with renewed vigour and appreciation. At that point, you can understand that you had to face hardship in order to value life. What was incomprehensible once becomes clear.

Another aspect of enlightenment is a lack of negative emotions. Perhaps this is what The Mouser is telling us when she speaks of questions and answers. If you do not sit in judgment on others or on your own life, but merely seek understanding, then no occurrence is negative or positive. It simply is what it is.

If you decide to embark on your spiritual journey, keep the lessons and stories of Yo Meow Ma in your heart. Her wisdom transcends time and species and is her special gift to you

Think not of the prey that escaped, but of the meals you ate.

———————————

The Story of Fu Tze

Fu Tze was a mischievous kitten who enjoyed playing tricks. He covered his tongue with the juice of red berries and offered to groom his sister, whose fur was white as the crane's feathers. When he had finished he howled for their mother, claiming his sister had been injured. His mother came running and there was panic in her eyes when she saw the kitten, looking painted with blood. Tze delighted at her distress. "You are a bad kitten," his mother scolded. "How would you feel if you thought your littermate had been hurt?" Tze knew she was unharmed, so he merely purred and walked away.

Tze's friends also fell prey to his mischief. One day, Tze covered his mouth with sea foam, then visited his best friend, Hau Ling. Ling feared that Tze had contracted the madness of rabies, and tried to escape. Tze caught him, and bit him on the neck. Thinking his life ended, Ling cowered and shook. When Ling realized it was a trick, he said, "You are a bad kitten. How would you feel if you thought you had been polluted with madness?" Tze knew he was not diseased, so he merely returned home.

When he reached the age of tom, Tze said goodbye to his mother and friends. "Please be wary of wolves," they said, for there were many packs roaming the few remaining territories. He waved away their cautions, saying he did not fear the wolves. He was smarter than a wolf, and could stop any aggression. He found a territory that was free of cats, had a source of water and fish, and a thriving community of pika. It was just the place for him. He marked the land with his scent and settled in for a long, happy life.

Two days later, he heard wolf howls near his den. Tze cowered beneath a thin bush that offered little protection — his territory had no trees.

He had nothing to climb, and nowhere to go. Panic stricken, he darted from the bush, running here and there, searching for safety. With the wolf howls closer than ever, he managed to squeeze into a burrow. As he lay quivering in the dark, cramped hole, he listened to the howls. There was something strange about them. They were not the howls of wolves, they were the howls of a cat pretending to be a wolf!

He called out to his tormentor and heard the familiar mew of Hau Ling. Angrily, Tze tried to leap out of the burrow. To his horror, and to the Ling's amusement, he was stuck. "Get me out!" he yowled.

"Why are you in a hole?" asked Ling.

"You are a bad cat!" Tze said. "How would you feel if you thought wolves were hunting you?"

"They weren't real wolves, so it does not matter," said Ling, and he left Tze in the hole.

A week passed before hunger thinned his body enough for Tze to squeeze out of the hole. Humbled, he returned to his mother, hoping she would seek revenge for what had happened to her son.

"When you treat other cats without respect, know that they will treat you in same manner," she said. "From this day forward, treat every cat you meet as you wish them to treat you.'

Tze took her words into his heart, and lived to be old and fat, his body filled with pika and his heart filled with friendships.

The Golden Rule, which is the moralistic heart of this teaching story, appears in some form or another in most major religions. From Christianity to Buddhism, from Islam to Hinduism, and many more besides, this one very basic rule of behavior – "Do unto others as you would have them do unto you" – is taught. It should not be surprising that a creature with the wisdom of Yo Meow Ma would have also discerned this universal truth.

If I were asked what my own life philosophy was, I would cite this venerable golden axiom. At heart, every human being on earth wants to be happy. It is the requirements for happiness, and not the goal, that separates us. Yet within all the particular ways in which we seek a joyous life, certain broad rules apply. It's not difficult to understand that if you wish to be treated in a certain way, according to your rules of happiness, that the best place to start is to treat others in a similar fashion.

The Golden Rule carries with it no guarantees. Everyone would have to adhere to it for it to be a certain road to happiness. But it does give you a fighting chance in a world filled with strangers, pitfalls, and unknown circumstances. Just as Tze learned the consequences of treating others without respect in a dangerous land, so could you if you abandon the Golden Rule. By treating everyone you meet as you want them to treat you, your world has the potential to be bereft of enemies and filled with friends.

Even if you spend all nine lives
trying to have everything,
you still die with nothing.